HAPPINESS HABITS

A JOURNAL FOR BUILDING SMALL, EASY HABITS FOR MINDFULNESS, HAPPINESS, AND SUCCESS

EVA OLSEN

author of *The One-Minute Happiness Journal*
and *Little Lists for a Happy Life*

CASTLE POINT BOOKS
NEW YORK

Krusty Krab

CONTENTS

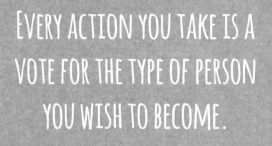

EVERY ACTION YOU TAKE IS A VOTE FOR THE TYPE OF PERSON YOU WISH TO BECOME.

—James Clear, *Atomic Habits*

INTRODUCTION

THERE IS NO ACTION TOO SMALL to change your day for the better. When times feel dark or overwhelming, the idea of "finding happiness" sounds like a search for buried treasure. Even if you had all the tools to cross a vast ocean and dig deep for your reward, where do you even get the map? But happiness doesn't have to be an impossible hunt—it's right in front of you, like tiny gemstones scattered along your path.

When you sprinkle even the smallest actions into your routine that make you feel more fulfilled, you slowly build good, rewarding habits that make you feel like you have found that treasure. Whether it's jotting down one thing that made you smile today, setting a daily reminder to take a deep cathartic breath at 12:01 p.m., sharing one nice memory a week with a loved one, or stretching for one minute in the morning, the repetition of those easy actions becomes an instinctual way to feel steady satisfaction.

Happiness Habits is your guide to collecting small joys, healthy patterns, and easy ways to feel accomplished that might appear insignificant on their own, but build big happiness together. Begin by nourishing the positive habits you already perform, slowly trim away the ones that do not serve you, and add new habits that empower and fulfill you. No more lifestyle overhauls, no annual resolutions that go unfulfilled—just easy, tiny habits that add to your happiness pile, one glittering gemstone at a time.

> # THE ONLY PERSON I KNOW,
> # IS THE PERSON I WANT TO BE.
>
> — Stephen R. Covey,
> *The 7 Habits of Highly Effective People*

POWER SOURCE.
What about these accomplishments would make you feel most fulfilled?

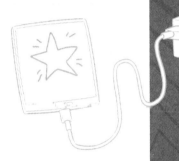

BANISH THE DEMONS.
What do you perceive to be the biggest obstacles?

WHOM DO YOU ADMIRE MOST?
Write down one thing they do that you wish to emulate.

A DAY IN THE LIFE.
Name one thing that person does that you do, too,
or a characteristic they have that you share.

GOALS. GOALS. GOALS. What are the big goals you have already set for yourself that you struggle to accomplish?

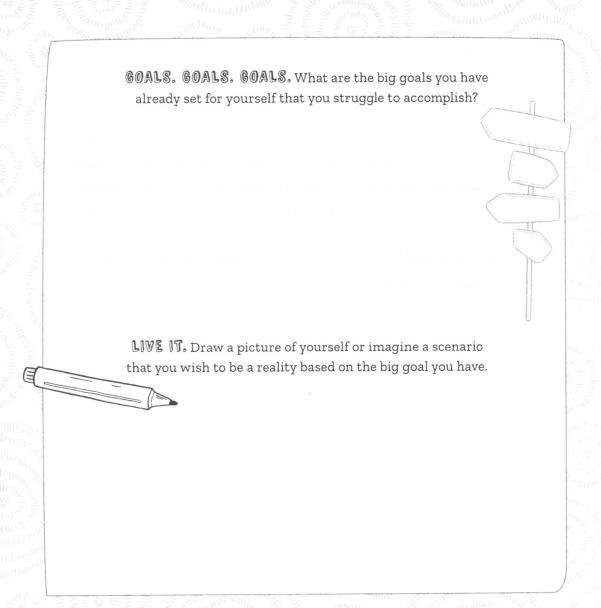

LIVE IT. Draw a picture of yourself or imagine a scenario that you wish to be a reality based on the big goal you have.

LIVE IN THAT GOOD FEELING.

For what can you pat yourself on the back?

SMALL SCORE, BIG WIN. What is a little, barely noticeable part of the process that helped you achieve that accomplishment?

MAKE IT EASY. Don't ask yourself to go from zero to Iron Man or zero dollars to millions. What amount of effort would feel completely unnoticeable as the first step to doing something you'd like to do?

FEELING IT. What do you hope to feel when you set goals for yourself? Break it down. Rather than *I want to be successful*, it might be, *I want to have an impact on my colleagues.*

LITTLE SCORE! What tiny, itty-bitty step can you take to put your big goal into motion? If your big goal is hitting the gym, then your "little score" is putting on your workout clothes.

TWO POINTS! What is one habit you can add after you complete your little score that will propel you forward? If the first habit is putting on your workout clothes, the second could be drinking a glass of water right after.

IT'S OKAY TO WORRY. What are you worried about if you don't hit the big mark you're seeking?

HOW CAN YOU BE GENTLER WITH YOURSELF?
Write a note as if you were giving advice to a friend.

Draw a visual representation of the
TASK YOU LEAST WANT TO ATTACK.
Silly or scary, make it more familiar to you.

COURAGE IS YOURS.
Write out what you would say to it
in a moment of strength.

Imagine a world in which everything you want is handed to you.
How would you **GIVE BACK** to someone else?

Write a **STATEMENT OF GRATITUDE**
for how you would feel if you had it all.

HELPING HANDS.

Who helps you reach your goals?

WHAT IS ONE DEED

performed by someone else that helps you?

SCHEDULE THE PERFECT DAY. On the clock below, write in what you think your hours should look like.

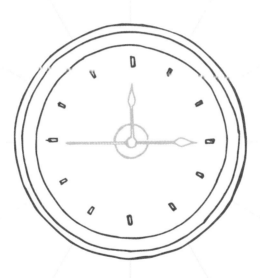

THAT'S IMPRESSIVE! Make a list of the most
awe-inspiring things you have ever seen.

WHAT ABOUT THESE

objects, moments, or forces of nature was so profound?

DRAW SOMETHING GOOD.

Describe what it means to have
GOOD HABITS.

WHO has them?

TODAY AND EVERY DAY.
What small action do you perform every day that brings you joy?

What do you know will happen every day that brings you a
SENSE OF RELIEF?

IT'S IN YOUR ENVIRONMENT.

What are the positive things around you
that make your life easier?

MAGIC WAND. What is one small change
you would make to improve your circumstances?

Draw what comes to mind when you think of the word
"CHALLENGE."

WRITE YOUR VICTORY SPEECH

for when you overcome it.

LUCKY NUMBER 7.

What are 7 habits you have
that make you feel good?

1.

2.

3.

4.

5.

6.

7.

HIGH FIVES!

Make a list of your most treasured accomplishments.

Was there a common denominator among
THESE TRIUMPHS?

What is **HAPPINESS** to you?

What things, people, or moments are
REQUIRED TO REACH IT?

ADMIRATION! Think of someone you admire.
Make a list of all their best quirks, qualities, or strengths.

WHAT BAD HABITS
do they have that you do not?

YOU'RE WELCOME. What are things you do out of habit
that are unintentionally helpful to others?

How do you **KNOW?**

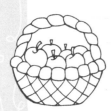

CULTIVATION.

Do you have any habits that you began deliberately?

What made you
CHOOSE TO START?

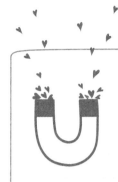

Who **ADMIRES** you?

What is one positive thing they might **SAY ABOUT YOU?**

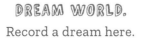

DREAM WORLD.

Record a dream here.

What about it makes you
FEEL BEST?

 **PAST TRIUMPHS.** Think of a recent success and list what was most helpful to you in reaching it.

If you ever felt stalled on your way there, what helped you **RESTART** your engine?

DESCRIBE A MOMENT
when you felt the most satisfaction.

What **SIGHTS, SOUNDS, FLAVORS, FEELINGS,** or **SMELLS** were present?

CHEERS.

If you were to give yourself a toast, what would you say?

Of what are you **MOST PROUD?**

What **MOTIVATES** you?

What **BORES** you?

WHAT keeps you going?

WHO lifts you up?

TODAY IS THE DAY YOU REACH A BIG GOAL.

What is one small thing you will do tomorrow
to make sure it's still real?

And the **NEXT DAY?**

THE HABITS I'VE COLLECTED ON MY PATH.

Write down the habits you already have about which you feel most positive. Track them for a week and describe how they make you feel.

HABIT

HOW IT MAKES ME SHINE

S M T W TH F S

S M T W TH F S

S M T W TH F S

S M T W TH F S

S M T W TH F S

S M T W TH F S

S M T W TH F S

S M T W TH F S

S M T W TH F S

MY OWN GOALS

Think more deeply about the habits you already have.
In what ways do they help you most along the way?

Stop judging yourself.
Take your aspirations and break
them down into tiny behaviors.
Embrace mistakes as discoveries
and use them to move forward.

— B. J. Fogg, *Tiny Habits*

BYE-BYE BAD HABITS

Sift through the subtle tendencies, vices, and not-so-great habits that don't do you any good. Think about why you are drawn to them, what they teach you, and whether you can toss them aside or let them tarnish from disuse. Use this section as an opportunity to reflect on and move away from what hasn't worked for you in the past.

EVERYONE HAS VICES.
What are yours?

RATE YOUR VICES on a scale from 1 to 10, with 1 indicating
a low level of negative impact on your world and 10 being highly negative.

VICE   NEGATIVE IMPACT

	1	2	3	4	5	6	7	8	9	10
	1	2	3	4	5	6	7	8	9	10
	1	2	3	4	5	6	7	8	9	10
	1	2	3	4	5	6	7	8	9	10
	1	2	3	4	5	6	7	8	9	10
	1	2	3	4	5	6	7	8	9	10
	1	2	3	4	5	6	7	8	9	10

DRAW A REPRESENTATION of how one of these vices makes you feel. (For example, if it's too much screen time, you could draw a zombie.)

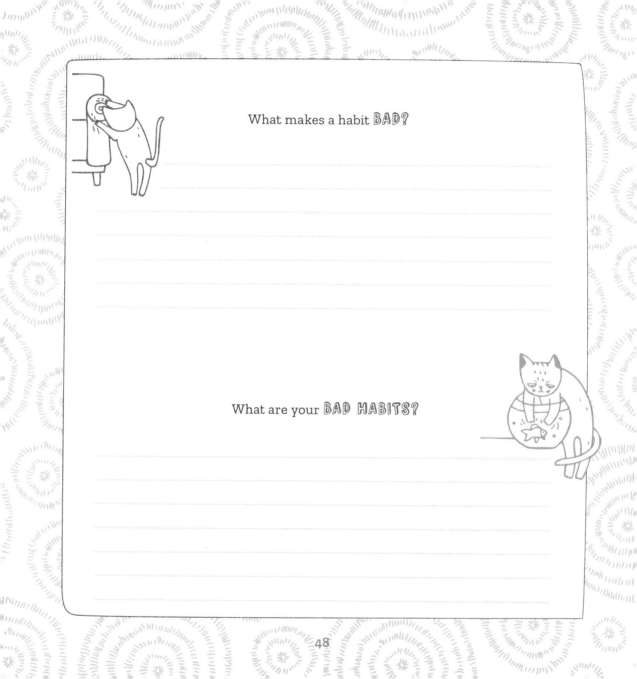

What makes a habit **BAD?**

What are your **BAD HABITS?**

Which bad habits
BOTHER YOU?

Which ones give you comfort
or make you **FEEL GOOD?**

WHAT ABOUT YOUR ENVIRONMENT
makes it easy to fall into these habits?

WHAT HAPPENS
right before you start them?

WHAT HABITS DO YOU HAVE
that someone else might say are bad,
but that you feel good about?

What makes them **FEEL THAT WAY?**

MAKING CHANGES.

Of all your bad habits, which ones do you most want to change?

Which ones are you happy
KEEPING?

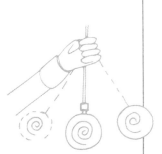

CHA-CHING.

What is the reward you get from them?

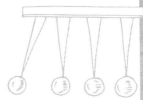

NEGATIVE BALANCE.

What is the fallout?

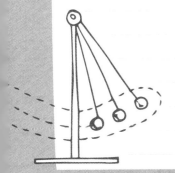

OLD FLAME.

What is it about these tendencies that makes them so hard to break?

What kind of DESIRE do you feel for them?

GRAB THE MEGAPHONE. Speak to your habits.
What do you want to say to them?

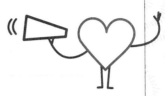

WHO SHARES the same habits?

THINK ABOUT THE FEELINGS YOU HAVE

immediately before and after you perform one of these actions.
If it's biting your nails, it might be stress before and relief after.

ACTION   FEELING

WHAT IS A SMALL ACTION

you could do instead to get similar results?

MAKE THEM HARD.

What would make your bad habits less convenient?

MAKE THEM UGLY.

What would make them less desirable?

FROM THE CHEAP SEATS,

Who is your biggest critic?

What about their criticism
MOST IRKS YOU?

HOLDING YOUR HAND.

Who is your biggest supporter?

WHEN HAS THAT PERSON ACCEPTED YOU,

even though what you were doing was bothersome?

SHOUT IT FROM THE MOUNTAINTOP.

Say farewell to some of these bad habits.

How do you **HOPE TO FEEL** without them?

YOU ARE YOUR BEST PARTNER.

Write some notes of support to yourself here.

CIRCLE THE SMILEY FACES.

Where do you land?

FOOL'S GOLD. Write down the habits you have about which you feel most negatively. Track them for a week and describe how they make you feel. Can you skip or replace any of them?

HABIT	WHEN I SKIPPED OR REPLACED THEM
	S M T W TH F S
	S M T W TH F S
	S M T W TH F S
	S M T W TH F S
	S M T W TH F S
	S M T W TH F S
	S M T W TH F S
	S M T W TH F S
	S M T W TH F S

MY OWN GOALS.

Think more deeply about the bad habits you perform.
How do they get in your way?

THIS IS THE REAL POWER OF HABIT:
THE INSIGHT THAT YOUR HABITS ARE
WHAT YOU CHOOSE THEM TO BE.

— Charles Duhigg, *The Power of Habit*

HELLO LITTLE, EASY HABITS

Let the little things catch your eye. Be on the lookout for incremental changes, easy adjustments, and tiny flecks of success that make you feel more fulfilled. This section allows you to pick up small habits that gradually help you rather than trying to haul large, unyielding ones.

PROMISES, PROMISES.

Skip the big oaths and resolutions. What promises have you made
to yourself in the past that ended up in disappointment?

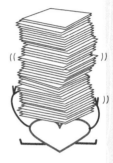

WHAT SMALLER, BABY PROMISE

could you have made that you'd be more likely to keep?

GRAINS OF SAND.

Every little bit counts. Break down the increments required to get to some of your larger goals. If your big goal is flossing every day, then one little action is buying floss. A second is placing it near your toothbrush.

CRYSTAL CLEAR. It's not always a lack of motivation
that gets in the way of good habits, but a fuzziness about how or
when to perform them. Concrete, clear actions help you take the first step.

IF IT INVOLVES GOING SOMEWHERE,
which *literal* route will you take?
Is someone else involved? Who?

ACTION	TIME	LOCATION

BIG TALK. When you think of your habits, rituals, or errands, what kind of language do you use?

INSTEAD OF SAYING
you *have* to do something, like meal prep,
say what you *get* to do, like provide your body with fuel.

WORDS OF ENCOURAGEMENT.
What positive language
could you use to describe your everyday actions?

HOORAY. What mini-celebrations
could you perform each time you do something small?

IDEALISM FOR REALISTS. Write down the first thing
you think you *should* do in the morning, like exercise for a half hour.

INSTEAD OF DOING THAT THING, do a version
that takes only 30 seconds to a minute, max. How does it feel?

DO IT AGAIN TOMORROW. And the next day.
Commit to this short window until it becomes second nature.
Write in smiley or frown faces based on how you felt about it.

| S | M | T | W | TH | F | S |

KEEP IT SHORT.
Even if you want to build a regular habit, like writing poetry
for an hour a day, start by giving yourself a mandatory cut-off time.
This amount of time should feel too short,
like 2 minutes or 5 minutes. What is it for you?

STACK IT! Easy habits are like stackable rings. Every one you have is nice on its own, but together they are something special you want to wear all the time. Imagine a series of tiny habits as stacking rings, like drinking a full glass of water while you wait for coffee to brew, then thinking of one thing you are grateful for while drinking your coffee, and then tidying one thing in your kitchen when you have finished your coffee.

Make sure these habits are super-easy on their own.
EACH ACTION IS A CUE for the next one, and then they become routine.

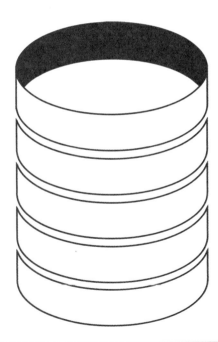

MINDFULNESS AND YOU.

What does mindfulness mean to you?

What is a seemingly **INSIGNIFICANT ACTION** you can perform to add it to your day?

WORK. WORK. WORK.

What is something you enjoy about your work?

WHAT IS ONE THING YOU DO REGULARLY

that makes your work life easier?

IN THE OFFICE. Name a tiny action that you could perform at work that could improve your day-to-day life. It could be taking an extra moment to ask a coworker how their day is going, or making a point of unsubscribing from the e-mails that fill up your inbox but you ordinarily just delete.

THIS FELT:

S	M	T	W	TH	F	S

HI, FRIEND!
What keeps your friendships strong?

What do you always do that makes you
FEEL CONNECTED?

FROM ME TO YOU. Create a new, teeny-tiny touchpoint to maintain a connection with friends, like sending a waving emoji or following up about the last thing they said to you.

How often could you remind people that
YOU ARE THINKING OF THEM?

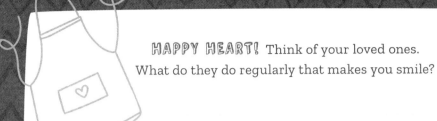

HAPPY HEART! Think of your loved ones.
What do they do regularly that makes you smile?

What do you do regularly to **MAKE THEM FEEL GOOD,**
like morning hugs or offering kernels of praise?

HEART FULL. Every day this week, fill in the degree to which your heart feels good. Whether it's seeing a video of a cute puppy or nice feedback from a coworker, each small event fills a little bit more of your heart.

WHY, THANK YOU. Choose a small way to show more gratitude to someone. This could be emotional gratitude or a little thank-you to someone with whom you've had a fleeting interaction.

YOU ARE MY SUNSHINE. In the sun below, write the names of all of the people who make you smile.

MY BODY, MYSELF.

Choose a way to appreciate your body
each day. Notice something that works without
any or much thought, like your beating heart or your wiggling toes.
What, if anything, amazes you about this?

DAY TRADING.

Trade a bad habit for a good one today. Which will you choose?

What did that SWITCHEROO mean for you?

BEAUTY ROUTINE. Set an alarm for one tiny action you'd like to do every day. This could be taking a big, deep breath, or a moment to step outside and look at one element of nature for 10 seconds.

RECORD WHAT YOU NOTICE.

GIVE YOURSELF A MENTAL BREAK.

What is your favorite way to decompress?
Can you make a point of doing it in small doses?

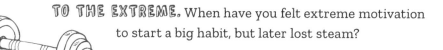

TO THE EXTREME. When have you felt extreme motivation to start a big habit, but later lost steam?

Could you have implemented a **SHORTER VERSION** of it, like 10 seconds of running in place, rather than running a mile?

WHAT GETS IN YOUR WAY
of what you would like to accomplish?

Draw how you might
DEFEAT THIS CHALLENGER.

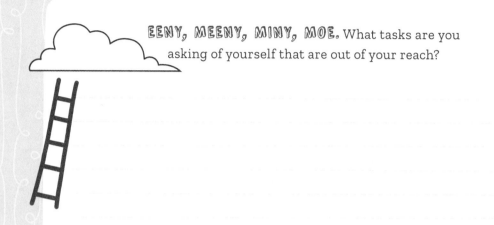

EENY, MEENY, MINY, MOE. What tasks are you asking of yourself that are out of your reach?

WHAT KIND OF HABITS

would take advantage of your skills or environment?

CONSTANT CRAVINGS. What habits are so ingrained that you get antsy if you don't do them?

What makes you **CRAVE** them?

EASY PEASY.

Make a list of things that are easy for you.

Of those things, which are
HARD FOR OTHERS?

MOUNTAIN TO CLIMB.
Draw yourself on the mountaintop.

WHAT do you see?

LITTLE TREASURES.

Create some of your own tiny routines.
Track them for a week and describe how they make you feel.

HABIT 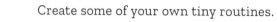 HOW IT MAKES ME SHIMMER

S   M   T   W   TH   F   S

S   M   T   W   TH   F   S

S   M   T   W   TH   F   S

S   M   T   W   TH   F   S

S   M   T   W   TH   F   S

S   M   T   W   TH   F   S

S   M   T   W   TH   F   S

S   M   T   W   TH   F   S

S   M   T   W   TH   F   S

MY OWN GOALS
Think more deeply about the habits you are forming.

How are they **MAKING YOU FEEL?**

I SHOULD PURSUE ONLY THOSE HABITS
THAT WOULD MAKE ME FEEL FREER
AND STRONGER.

— Gretchen Rubin, *Better Than Before*

HAPPINESS HABITS

Gather up those hopes and dreams and find new ways to let
them sparkle. Choose from different habits, behaviors, and
small actions that shine brightest for you and that you can
incorporate into your routine without difficulty. Cast off
the need for big wins, reduce the pressure you place on
yourself, and let satisfaction come by building small,
healthy, and achievable ways to feel good.

RISE AND SHINE. Take a calming moment in the morning to think about the day ahead. Set one intention for your day.

Sketch a moment of
HAPPINESS.

COUNT TO TEN. When your tensions begin to rise, list ten funny words to defuse your own fury. What are they?

IT'S WRITTEN IN THE STARS. Look up at the sky and accept a moment of wonder. What does this moment bring you?

LOOK FOR THE HELPERS. Who helps you with small things? It could be your coworker, your roommate, or the cashier at your favorite grocery store.

Write down one thing every day said by a friend.
WHAT STANDS OUT?

Do one thing you didn't do yesterday.
WHAT WILL YOU CHOOSE?

SET A TIMER FOR 60 SECONDS.

Close your eyes and take deep breaths as the time passes.
When the minute is up, jot down one word to describe how you feel.

Write your *"BURIED TREASURE" GOAL* on one side of this page, and your *"GEMSTONE" HABIT* on the other. If building new friendships is your big goal, then your tiny habit could be sending a text or waving hello to a stranger.

Draw an **ELEMENT OF NATURE** that brings you peace.

BIG WORDS, BIG WISDOM.

Write a quotation, lyric, or saying that makes you feel energized.

READ SOMETHING OUT OF YOUR COMFORT ZONE.

Choose a short passage from a writer, news source, or expert that you would normally pass over. What makes you uncomfortable?

WHAT DRAWS YOU IN?

SAY HELLO TO A FRIEND.
What kinds of encouragement might
a friend need that you can provide?

TAKE A MOMENT TO STRETCH when stress is getting high.
Feel the energy from your fingertips to your toes. Take slow breaths to give
yourself some mental space from the stress and describe how this feels.

SCORE!
Count your small wins today.

For what are you **NOT GIVING YOURSELF** enough credit?

SMILES FOR MILES. When something makes you smile, hold on to it for an extra moment. What does it mean to you?

How does **SOMEONE ELSE'S SMILE** affect you?

SHUT IT DOWN. When something or someone upsets you, what is one thing you can do to center yourself?

Write down an **ENCOURAGING QUOTATION** or mantra for when you need a boost.

you are awesome

TRY SOMETHING NEW. Choose one thing to mix up your day that you wouldn't normally do. What is it?

RATE IT on a scale of 1 to 10.

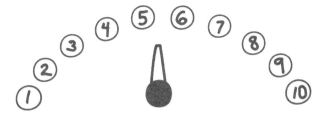

SWEAT. Move your body with high intensity for 5 minutes a day and write your reactions.

Which of these would **WORK FOR YOU?**

SWAYING YOUR ARMS   HULA-HOOPING

DANCING   LIFTING WEIGHTS

SPEED WALKING   CLIMBING

A 5-MINUTE WORKOUT APP   RUNNING

PLAY A SONG IN A FOREIGN LANGUAGE.

What can you decipher?

Can you find a **PERSONAL CONNECTION**—whether from the rhythm of the music or the sound of the singer's voice—that makes you understand?

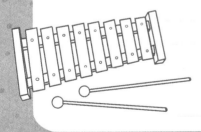

SPEAK YOUR GRATITUDE. Express gratitude to one person a day. How has one person reacted?

Write a **THANK-YOU NOTE** to someone you have never met.

IT'S YOUR STORY. Write for 1 minute a day, adding to a story of your own invention. What is your first line?

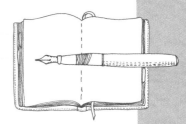

What **INSPIRES** you?

OFF THE GRID. Limit your biggest distractions. How does it feel if you put your phone away or turn off the Internet when you need to focus?

HOW MANY MINUTES A DAY
can you schedule this silence?

LISTEN TO SOMEONE YOU DON'T LIKE. Whether it's an in-person interaction or someone on social media, what comes from just listening?

What about them **BOTHERS YOU MOST?**

MAKE YOUR TASKS FEEL SMALLER.

If you have a big work project, what's the first, incremental step in starting it?

Decide what your **PICK-ME-UP PHRASE** will
be when you are feeling discouraged:

CELEBRATE SELF-CARE.

What is your go-to act of self-care?

If it's not something you can do every day,
HOW FREQUENTLY CAN YOU SCHEDULE IT?

MINDFUL MOMENT.

Choose one person in your life and send them good wishes here:

WRITE A GOOD WISH for yourself.

HELP SOMEONE TODAY. Make a point of taking an extra moment to show someone you can help. What will it be?

What are the **STRENGTHS YOU OFFER** that can be helpful to someone else?

POST IT! Keep a stash of cards and stamps in a drawer for a rainy day, friends' birthdays, or special occasions. Who in your life would benefit most from a handwritten note?

ONE MOMENT EVERY DAY.

Take a short video every day and, after a while, edit them together into a longer video. What does the act of capturing little moments bring you?

ACCEPT CRITICISM MORE OFTEN. When someone critiques you, write it down and come back to it later. What sticks with you? What do you need to discard?

SHOW AUTHENTICITY. Make one tally of the occasions when you notice yourself being insincere and another of when you show earnestness.

QUALITY OVER QUANTITY. Take stock of your most meaningful connections. What does tending to these deeper relationships add that is more rewarding than trying to please lots of people?

COLOR IN the garden below.

UNPLUG. When you are burned out, don't continue to fry. What will your go-to be to recharge when you need it most?

SLEEP. Set a timer in your phone for when you should go to bed. Record your sleep times for the week here.

How does tracking your sleep patterns **HELP YOUR RESTFULNESS?**

TAKE A BREAK. Force yourself to
step away from work, even if you don't feel
that you need a break. What activity could you do
for a few minutes that won't feel like work?
What time will you do this?

ACTIVITY   TIME

SCATTER COMPLIMENTS. Make a point
of saying something nice that you believe to be true
to someone each day. What will you say?
How does the receiver of your compliment react?

COMPLIMENT

REACTION

MESSAGE IN A BOTTLE.

Write thank-you notes you won't send. Write them to the people who have hurt you as a reflection of how they made you grow. Who are your recipients?

How can you take more personal time to be
THOUGHTFUL ABOUT HARD THINGS?

DO SOMETHING LUXURIOUS.

Make a point of treating yourself at various intervals.

What would make you feel best?

When will you schedule it?

MAKE PLAYLISTS FOR YOUR MOODS.
How can indulging in the sounds of your soul help you?

WHAT LYRICS OR MELODIES
stand out to you most?

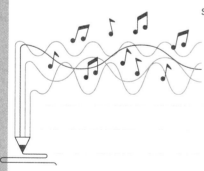

BELLY LAUGHS.

What small moments of laughter can you inspire in your day?

In what ways can you
CREATE MORE SMILES AND LAUGHTER for someone else?

SIMPLIFY. Trim away the things
that don't bring you happiness or are no longer useful to you.
What do you keep around that you could discard or give away?

Start with one now, and describe
HOW LETTING GO FEELS TO YOU.

RAGE PAGE.

Recognize when you are feeling sad or angry and find more stabilizing crutches to lean on.

Use this box to scribble out
YOUR FRUSTRATIONS.

UNFOLLOW!

Unfriend or unfollow the people or pages that make you feel dread.
How does it feel to go without seeing them?

FOLLOW SOMETHING POSITIVE INSTEAD.

What pages can you start viewing that will be
better for your emotional health?

SAY IT OUT LOUD. Don't let your feelings get bottled up.
Even if it is to the open air, release your thoughts.
What are you most likely to say?

LIGHT CANDLES.
How does sitting with something soothing help
when you are stressed?

LISTEN TO THE SOUNDS OF NATURE.

Choose one way to celebrate nature each day.

Listen to the wind, a body of water, or the sounds of birds.

What does stopping to listen mean for you?

DRAW what you hear.

GET OUT OF YOUR COMFORT ZONE.

Make an effort to do something you wouldn't ordinarily do.
Who could be your accountability ally? What will you do first?

MAKE A LIST of the things
that seemed scary at first but led to a reward.

CONSIDER THE HABITS of a valued mentor or coworker.
Which ones would you also like to take on?

WHICH OF THESE HABITS are out of your reach,
but could inspire another activity?

DRAW your most confident self.

WRITE what you are thinking in this image.

ACKNOWLEDGE yourself for your hard work.
How will you reward yourself when something goes well?

BE HONEST when something fails. How can you turn a
disappointment into something you can appreciate?

PRACTICE SPEAKING to yourself with more kindness.
What words do you usually use that are negative?

WHAT LANGUAGE can you use that is more compassionate?

TIDY HOUSE. If cleaning is hard for you, what's one little thing you can do that *maintains* the space that you barely notice?

What's another thing you can **ADD TO THIS PROCESS?**

GOODNIGHT, SWEETHEART.
What is your ideal way to put yourself to bed?
What kinds of cozy comforts can you add more regularly for better rest?

IN YOUR DREAMS. Keep a notepad next to your bed. When you wake up after a dream, record your notes before falling back to sleep. How might analyzing your dreams help?

SHOW SOME LOVE.

What daily actions can you take
to be loving to someone you care about?

Who is the person who **NEEDS YOUR LOVE** the most?

REFRAME YOUR THINKING ABOUT FAILURE. When something goes wrong, consider that it reached its natural life span. What things have you thought of as failures but that sprouted something else?

When a relationship ends, **HOW WILL YOU HONOR IT?** Worry less about grudges and think more about the perspective it brings you.

EXPRESS YOUR LOVE LANGUAGES MORE.

How do you best express and receive love?

How can you be more proactive about loving?

LOVE IN RETURN.

Find out how other people you care about want to be loved.

How can you use what they have told you to show them you care?

LEARN SOMETHING NEW.
In what ways can you be more open to learning?

What INSPIRES your FOCUS?

GO PLACES. Whether it's across town or across the globe, make a point to leave your bubble. Where will you go? What do you hope to find?

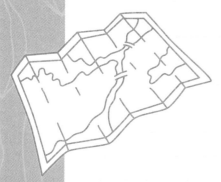

DRAW a map of your next destination, or a picture of your next adventure.

PUSH YOURSELF. Choose one thing that doesn't feel comfortable but you know will be good for you. How does it feel to put the first foot forward?

BE OPEN TO NEW FRIENDSHIPS.
Who is an unlikely candidate for your pool of friends?
In what ways could you reach out to new people?

BE GENEROUS.

How can you be more generous with your time, your heart, or something someone else might need more? When can you be generous next?

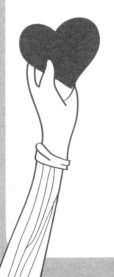

How has someone been GENEROUS TO YOU?

PRACTICE FORGIVENESS. Even if it's just to yourself,
take note of the moments when you think you could be forgiving.
How do you plan to express it?

LET IT GO. Scatter your worries into the wind.
What kind of ritual can you perform when you
need a symbolic gesture of letting go?

FILL YOUR BODY WITH GOOD FUEL.

Set up your environment so you don't have to make the choice between something you are trying to avoid and something you think would be better for you. What do you keep within reach?

Drink a full glass of water when you wake up.
Keep track of it here and rate whether it makes you feel
HALF EMPTY OR HALF FULL.

STOP TORTURING YOURSELF.

Schedule appointments with yourself to be your own biggest supporter,
to show yourself compassion, and to treat yourself less critically.

WHAT NOTES OF ENCOURAGEMENT

do you think you may want to hear?

BETTER, NOT PERFECT. Don't get so caught up in success. How can you reward yourself for the process more regularly?

WHAT CAN YOU TELL YOURSELF if something doesn't go as planned?

TELL THE PEOPLE YOU LOVE THAT YOU LOVE THEM.

Schedule it or make it a regular way to sign off on a message,
phone call, or e-mail. To whom should you be saying it?

MAKE KINDNESS A RITUAL. How can you
be kinder to the people around you?

FLECKS OF GOLD. Collect some of your favorite Happiness Habits from this chapter. Track them over the long term and describe how they make you feel.

HABIT   HOW IT MAKES ME SHINE

S   M   T   W   TH   F   S

S   M   T   W   TH   F   S

S   M   T   W   TH   F   S

S   M   T   W   TH   F   S

S   M   T   W   TH   F   S

S   M   T   W   TH   F   S

S   M   T   W   TH   F   S

S   M   T   W   TH   F   S

S   M   T   W   TH   F   S

HABIT   HOW IT MAKES ME SHINE

S   M   T   W   TH   F   S

S   M   T   W   TH   F   S

S   M   T   W   TH   F   S

S   M   T   W   TH   F   S

S   M   T   W   TH   F   S

S   M   T   W   TH   F   S

S   M   T   W   TH   F   S

S   M   T   W   TH   F   S

S   M   T   W   TH   F   S

S   M   T   W   TH   F   S

S   M   T   W   TH   F   S

HABIT HOW IT MAKES ME SHINE

S   M   T   W   TH   F   S

S   M   T   W   TH   F   S

S   M   T   W   TH   F   S

S   M   T   W   TH   F   S

S   M   T   W   TH   F   S

S   M   T   W   TH   F   S

S   M   T   W   TH   F   S

S   M   T   W   TH   F   S

S   M   T   W   TH   F   S

S   M   T   W   TH   F   S

S   M   T   W   TH   F   S

HABIT

HOW IT MAKES ME SHINE

S M T W TH F S

S M T W TH F S

S M T W TH F S

S M T W TH F S

S M T W TH F S

S M T W TH F S

S M T W TH F S

S M T W TH F S

S M T W TH F S

S M T W TH F S

S M T W TH F S

HABIT

HOW IT MAKES ME SHINE

S   M   T   W   TH   F   S

S   M   T   W   TH   F   S

S   M   T   W   TH   F   S

S   M   T   W   TH   F   S

S   M   T   W   TH   F   S

S   M   T   W   TH   F   S

S   M   T   W   TH   F   S

S   M   T   W   TH   F   S

S   M   T   W   TH   F   S

S   M   T   W   TH   F   S

S   M   T   W   TH   F   S

HABIT   HOW IT MAKES ME SHINE

S   M   T   W   TH   F   S

S   M   T   W   TH   F   S

S   M   T   W   TH   F   S

S   M   T   W   TH   F   S

S   M   T   W   TH   F   S

S   M   T   W   TH   F   S

S   M   T   W   TH   F   S

S   M   T   W   TH   F   S

S   M   T   W   TH   F   S

S   M   T   W   TH   F   S

S   M   T   W   TH   F   S

HABIT

HOW IT MAKES ME SHINE

S M T W TH F S

S M T W TH F S

S M T W TH F S

S M T W TH F S

S M T W TH F S

S M T W TH F S

S M T W TH F S

S M T W TH F S

S M T W TH F S

S M T W TH F S

S M T W TH F S

HABIT

HOW IT MAKES ME SHINE

S   M   T   W   TH   F   S

S   M   T   W   TH   F   S

S   M   T   W   TH   F   S

S   M   T   W   TH   F   S

S   M   T   W   TH   F   S

S   M   T   W   TH   F   S

S   M   T   W   TH   F   S

S   M   T   W   TH   F   S

S   M   T   W   TH   F   S

S   M   T   W   TH   F   S

S   M   T   W   TH   F   S

About the Author

Eva Olsen lives the good life in Fort Collins, Colorado. Her husband, twin sons, hiking with friends, and the art of hand lettering bring her much happiness. She is the author of My Little Lykke Journal, Little Lists for a Happy Life, *and* The One-Minute Happiness Journal.